Welcome to the National Botanic Gardens, Glasnevin

left: *Paphiopedilum* 'General Wavell' centre: *Rosa* 'Bloomsday' right: *Romneya coulteri*

The National Botanic Gardens, Glasnevin, have been developed over two centuries. Many thousands of species of plants from a wide range of habitats and climatic regions are grown in addition to artificial hybrids and garden varieties.

The purpose of the plant collections has always been to stimulate an interest in the plant kingdom as well as to provide materials for demonstration, study and research in botany and horticulture. In addition to these traditional roles the Gardens are working actively for conservation by growing, propagating a   e or threatened with extinction.

This is not a comprehensive guide but is intended as an introduction to the history, purpose and nature of the Gardens. I hope that it will prove a useful memento of a pleasant visit.

Donal Synnott
Director.
(July 2000)

CONTENTS

opposite: Curvilinear Range *photo: Brendan Fogarty*

HISTORY

In 1790, the Irish Parliament, with the active support of The Speaker of the House, John Foster, granted funds to the Dublin Society (now the Royal Dublin Society), to establish a public botanic garden. In 1795, the Gardens were founded on lands at Glasnevin. The portrait of John Foster by William Beechey (1813) in Leinster House shows him sitting at his desk holding a map of the Botanic Gardens.

The original purpose of the Gardens was to promote a scientific approach to the study of agriculture. In its early years the Gardens demonstrated plants that were useful for animal and human food and medicine and for dyeing but it also grew plants that promoted an understanding of systematic botany or were simply beautiful or interesting in themselves. By the 1830's, the agricultural purpose of the Gardens had been overtaken by the pursuit of botanical knowledge. This was facilitated

John Foster
Photo: Michael Quinn. Reproduced by kind permission of The Oireachtas and the Royal Dublin Society

by the arrival of plants from around the world and by closer contact with the great gardens in Britain, notably Kew and Edinburgh and plant importers such as Messrs. Veitch. By 1838, the basic shape of the Gardens had been established. Ninian Niven as Curator had in four years laid out the system of roads and paths and located many of the garden features that are present today.

The ever increasing plant collection and especially plants from tropical areas demanded more and more protected growing conditions and it was left to Niven's successor, David Moore, to develop the glasshouse accommodation. Richard Turner, the great Dublin ironmaster, had already supplied an iron house to Belfast Gardens and he persuaded the Royal Dublin Society that such a house would be a better investment than a wooden house. So indeed it has proved.

Sir Frederick Moore

Glasnevin. The collections at Kilmacurragh, Headford and Fota, for example, attest to this.

It was David Moore who first noted potato blight in Ireland at Glasnevin on 20th August 1845 and predicted that the impact on the potato crop would lead to famine in Ireland. He continued to investigate the cause of the blight and correctly identified it as a fungus but narrowly missed finding a remedy.

David Moore was succeeded by his son Frederick, who was made Curator at the age of twenty-two. Some of the gardening establishment figures of the day were sceptical that such a young man would be up to the job. Frederick Moore soon justified his appointment and went on to establish Glasnevin as one of the great gardens of the world. In due course he was knighted for his services to horticulture.

The scientific purpose of the Gardens was overshadowed by its horticultural reputation during Frederick Moore's term of office. The Scientific Superintendent of the Gardens, William Ramsay McNab, died in 1889 and was not replaced. This hiatus lasted until the appointment of a Plant Taxonomist in 1968 and the transfer of the National Herbarium with two botanists from the National Museum in 1970.

A Development Plan for the Gardens, published in 1992, led to a dramatic programme of restoration and renewal. Primary amongst these was the magnificent restoration of the Turner Curvilinear Range of glasshouses completed for the bicentenary of the Gardens in 1995. A new purpose-built herbarium/library was

David Moore's contribution to the Gardens, to its plant collections and to its reputation nationally and internationally is unsurpassed. His interests and abilities were wide ranging; he had studied the flora of Antrim and Derry, fungi, algae, lichens, bryophytes, ferns and flowering plants, before taking up his post at Glasnevin. While at Glasnevin he developed links with Botanic Gardens in Britain, in Europe and in Australia (his brother Charles became Director at Sydney). Moore used the great interest in plants that existed among the estate owners and owners of large gardens in Ireland to expand trial grounds for rare plants not expected to thrive at

Curvilinear range

opened in 1997. The 18th century Director's House and the Curator's House have been refurbished. New service glasshouses and compost storage bays have been built. Additional lecture rooms for the Teagasc Course in Amenity Horticulture were opened in 1999. Improved visitor and education facilities have been provided in a new Visitor Centre. In tandem with the restoration and expansion of the buildings, upgrading of the collections and displays has also been in progress. The work of plant identification and classification, of documenting, labelling and publishing continues, as does that of education and service to the visiting public.

The Botanic Gardens came into State care in 1878 and since then have been administered variously by the Departments of Art and Industry, the Department of Agriculture and the Office of Public Works (OPW). Dúchas The Heritage Service of the Department of Arts, Heritage Gaeltacht and the Islands now have responsibility for the Gardens.

It is the stated purpose of Dúchas, "To enrich the quality of life and sense of identity of all our citizens and to preserve our inheritance for present and future generations".

opposite: The Pond below Pine Hill *photo: Brendan Fogarty*

TREES

right: The Addison Walk
(*Taxus baccata*)

above: *Davidia involucrata* 'Chinese handkerchief tree'

There are many hundreds of notable trees throughout the grounds as well as those concentrated in the arboretum at the western end of the Gardens.

The oldest trees are the native yews (*Taxus baccata*) in the avenue commemorating the essayist, Joseph Addison, who had been Secretary to the Lord Lieutenant in Ireland at the beginning of the 18th century. One ring-count indicates that they were planted before 1740. It is likely that they were planted by Thomas Tickell who was Addison's biographer and friend and who lived in what is now the Director's house at Glasnevin until his death in 1736. Tickell had been a Don at Oxford where there is also an Addison's Walk, though it is not defined by yew trees.

There is a fine specimen of the Irish yew (*Taxus baccata* 'Fastigiata') in front of the Curvilinear Glasshouse. The Irish yew is an upright form of the native tree with juvenile foliage that was discovered near Florence Court in County Fermanagh about 1740.

The yew collection, on the southern side of Pine Hill includes an old tree of the yellow-berried yew (*Taxus baccata* 'Lutea') which was donated to the Gardens in 1830 having been propagated from a plant originally growing at Clontarf Castle, Co. Dublin.

above: *Cornus capitata* at pond

above: *Liriodendron tulipifera*

Two Chusan palms (*Trachycarpus fortunei*) survive where they were planted out as an experiment in 1870. It was not known then if they would be hardy. One is in front of the Curvilinear Range, the other at the rear of the Director's House.

A Caucasian elm (*Zelkova carpinifolia*) in front of the Herbarium/Library building is the finest in Ireland.

Near the pond the Chinese handkerchief tree (*Davidia involucrata*) is beautiful in early May. It is associated with Augustine Henry who introduced many Chinese plants to the Western world and for whom *Emmenopterys henryi* is named. *Emmenopterys* is planted at the eastern end of the pond. Nearby is one of the tallest trees in the gardens, a Giant redwood (*Sequoiadendron giganteum*) from California. A multi-stemmed plant of the Giant redwood dominates the lawn in front of the Curvilinear Range. At the corner of the Range near the Succulent House is a fine form of the native Strawberry tree, Crann caithne (*Arbutus unedo*). This Mediterranean species grows wild in South West Ireland and about Lough Gill in County Sligo. It produces its flowers in October as the strawberry-like fruits from the previous year's flowers are maturing.

Other notable specimens include the Tree of Heaven (*Ailanthus altissima*) from China and the hybrid Strawberry tree (*Arbutus x andrachnoides*) near the Palm House, *Paulownia tomentosa* in the Chinese shrubbery, Dawn redwood (*Metasequoia glyptostroboides*) and Swamp cypress (*Taxodium distichum*) at the pond, Austrian pine (*Pinus nigra*) near the shattered Cedar of Lebanon (*Cedrus libani*) to the south of the Herbaceous Borders and *Maytenus boaria* at the end of the peony border.

The sculpture, 'Craobh', commissioned from Gerard Cox by the Royal Dublin Society and OPW for the bicentenary of the Gardens in 1995 is fashioned from the trunk of a fine Hungarian oak (*Quercus frainetto*) which succumbed to honey fungus in the 1980's.

above: *Prunus yedoensis*

9

SHRUBS

left: *Rosa chinensis* 'Old Blush' centre: *Paeonia suffruticosa* right: *Rosa* 'Easlea's Golden Rambler'

The shrub collections are generally arranged in botanical groups – for example Japanese quince, *Chaenomeles* species and cultivars, are grown near the Herbarium/Library. However, some shrubs are grown in geographical groups – there is the Chinese shrubbery and a New Zealand border. The main flush of bloom on hardy shrubs is in May but there are shrubs in bloom at Glasnevin throughout the year. From early January tasselbush (*Garrya elliptica*), witch hazels (*Hamamelis*), *Viburnum farreri, Sarcococca* and some *Mahonia* are in flower. The Cornelian cherry (*Cornus mas*) is covered in tiny yellow flowers and the crimson anthers of the Persian ironwood (*Parrotia persica*) are produced in February. *Forsythia, Rhododendron,* flowering currant (*Ribes*), Japanese quince (*Chaenomeles*), *Magnolia,* early *Clematis,* Japanese cherries (*Prunus spp.*), *Viburnum,* and *Corylus* produce colourful displays in March and April.

Glasnevin is renowned for its wall shrubs and many rare species can be found trained against the warmer walls.

above: *Chaenomeles x superba* 'Rowallane Seedling'
right: *Wisteria sinensis* photo: D Synnott

The late summer and autumn flowering shrubs include the Southern Hemisphere genus, *Eucryphia* – there is a fine young plant of *Eucryphia x nymansensis* 'Mount Usher' near the entrance.

The collection of *Cotoneaster* species in the National Botanic Gardens contains several rare plants, including *Cotoneaster bradyi*, named for a former Director, Aidan Brady.

Rosa chinensis is an ancient garden rose, long cultivated in China. *Rosa chinensis* 'Old Blush' was donated in 1950 by the Thomas Moore Society. It came from the plant at Jenkinstown House, Kilkenny, that, according to tradition, was the rose that inspired the famous song, the 'Last Rose of Summer'.

THE HERBACEOUS BORDERS

right: *Dianella tasmanica*

above: *Althaea rosea*

The large curving double herbaceous borders between the Camellia/Flowering House and the Rock Garden were first planted in the mid-19th century before herbaceous plantings were popularised by William Robinson and Gertrude Jekyl. They contain plants of interest all year round but are at their most spectacular in high summer when the full range of herbaceous perennials have grown to their maximum extent.

13

opposite: Herbaceous Borders *photo: Brendan Fogarty*

above: Tulips in semi-circular beds

above: *Eremurus robustus*

above: *Gentiana punctata*

Other interesting borders of herbaceous perennials are planted along the millrace and by the beech hedge surrounding the Director's House.

Specialist borders of *Salvia, Penstemon, Iris, Peonia* and *Potentilla* are also grown: *Salvia* on the south side of the Herbarium/Library building, Iris to the West, *Penstemon* on the approach to the Fern House, *Paeonia* and *Potentilla* near the Vine Border.

THE ROCK GARDEN

A large Stone Pine (*Pinus pinea*) from the Mediterranean dominates the rock garden. Other prominent plants include the slow growing conifer, *Cedrus libani* 'Comte de Dijon' and two venerable Japanese maples. The rock area includes a small scree surrounded by plantings of rhododendron and azalea and other plants of the heather family. A larger, open scree has been developed between and rock garden and the Curvilinear Range. Spring bulbs include naturalised *Crocus, Scilla* and *Chionodoxa*.

Mountain plants and plants of poor soils in other habitats from around the world are grown in island beds, each representing a particular part of the world. Here also can be seen *Lavandula* 'Glasnevin' and the controversially named *Zauschneria californica* 'Dublin'.

above: *Viola* 'Padparadja'

above: *Tulipa lanata*
left: *Dodecatheon hendersonii*
far left: The Rock Garden path

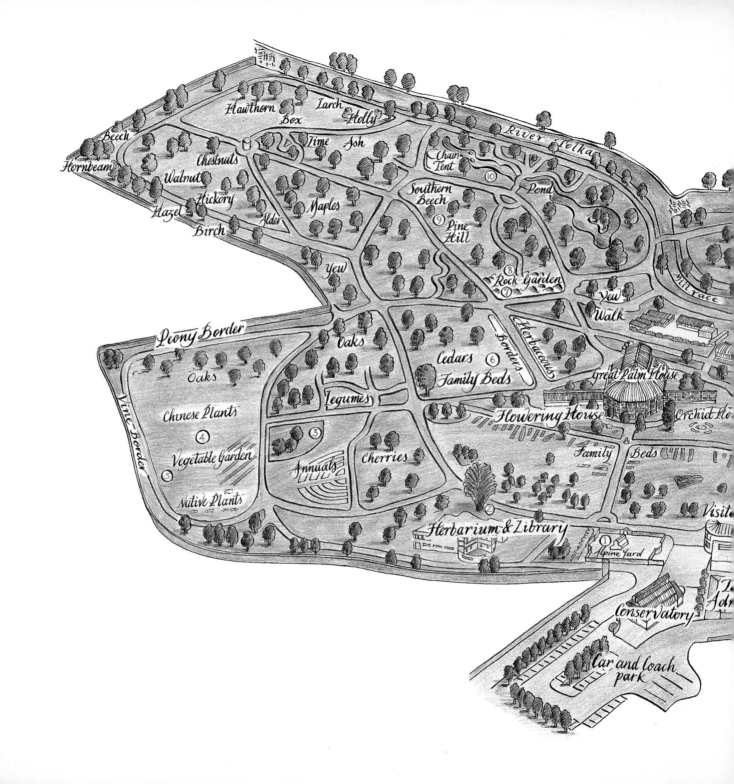

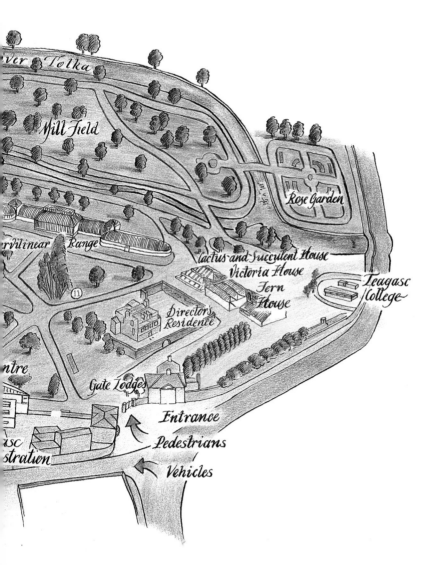

AREA
19.5 hectares (approx. 48 acres);
original area 16 Irish acres (1795)

LATITUDE
52° 22' North

LONGITUDE
06°16' West

GRID REFERENCE
O 1537

ALTITUDE
approx. 20m asl

PRECIPITATION
724 mm (mean annual, 1951-1980)

TEMPERATURE
mean January minimum 1.7°C
mean July maximum 19.3°C

absolute minimum -18.5°C
(12 January 1982)
absolute maximum 27.8°C

SOIL
sandy, lime-rich loam overlying gravel,
glacial and alluvial in origin; pH 7.5;
drainage excellent.

1. Alpine House

2. *Zelkova carpinifolia* (ironwood)

3. Magnolia Collection

4. Herb Garden

5. The Burren Garden

6. *Gymnocladus dioica* (Kentucky coffee tree)

7. *Cedrus libani* 'Comte de Dijon'

8. *Pinus pinea* (stone pine)

9. *Cedrus atlantica* 'Pendula' (weeping cedar)

10. *Metasequoia glyptostroboides* (dawn redwood)

11. *Sequoiadendron giganteum* (giant redwood)

THE CURVILINEAR RANGE

This beautiful range of glasshouses was manufactured, and for the most part built, by the great Dublin ironmaster, Richard Turner. The project began in 1843 and its first phase was completed in time for the visit of Queen Victoria to Ireland in 1849. The East and West wings of the house were doubled in size in 1868 and the low elegant turrets ingeniously inserted by Turner and his son William.

A widely acclaimed true restoration of the house was carried out by OPW in time for the bicentenary of the Gardens in 1995. The Europa Nostra Award for innovation in faithful restoration of a historic building was awarded in 1997.

The East Wing contains plants from South African Fynbos and from warm temperate parts of Western Australia and South America.

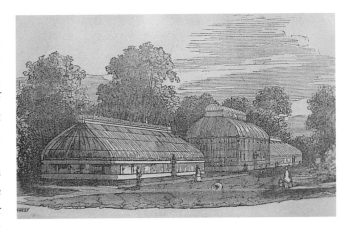

Above: The Curvilinear Range in 1850, as illustrated in a Garden guide of that date

left: *Conicosa pugioniformis* centre: *Eucalyptus macrocarpa* right: *Banksia serrata*

opposite: The Vireya rhododendron collection inside the Curvilinear Range

above: Tree ferns (*Dicksonia antarctica*) in West Wing
right: *Agapetes variegata* var. *macrantha*
far right: *Rhododendron polyanthemum*
bottom: *Rhododendron superbum*

The West Wing contains a collection of Vireya rhododendrons from tropical-montane South East Asia. This collection was gifted to the Gardens by the Royal Botanic Garden, Edinburgh.

Landscaping of the East and West Wings was designed by David Mitchell, Curator of Glasshouse collections at Edinburgh and carried out by Glasnevin and Edinburgh staff and students, a happy example of the co-operation and support of Botanic Gardens for each other.

In the central part of the house, too small for its original use as a palm house, a collection of conifer related plants – Gymnosperms – are grown to illustrate the evolution of that valuable part of the plant kingdom. The collection includes specimens of the primitive plant group, cycads, generously donated to Glasnevin by the Royal Botanic Gardens, Kew.

THE FLOWERING HOUSE

The house contains selections of houseplants and decorative plants in season – colour and scent to delight the eye and the nostril and to gladden the heart. For a number of years this house held the temperate plants from the Curvilinear Range while restoration of that house was in progress. Its original function as a flowering house has now been reinstated.

above: *Canna indica*   below: *Salvia involucrata*

below: Flowering House

THE ALPINE HOUSE AND YARD

left: *Lachenalia hybrida*　centre: *Corydalis flexuosa* 'China Blue'　right: *Primula aureata*

Alpine plants are, strictly speaking, plants which occur in the Alps or, by association, plants of the higher parts of mountain ranges throughout the world. For the generality of gardeners, however, the term has come to mean any small or low growing plants that are suitable for growing in small pots or in the rock garden.

Plants from a variety of habitats are grown in the Alpine Yard and House at Glasnevin. While many of the plants are indeed true alpines, others may be from sand dunes or coastal rocks of Europe, from the prairies of North America or from the Fynbos regions of South Africa. The Alpine House is kept supplied with interesting specimens from the large and growing collection in the Garden's Nursery. Hardy plants are often grown indoors to achieve better flowering or to prevent damage by the weather or by birds, slugs and snails.

Raised beds and troughs in the Alpine Yard are planted with small, choice specimens which would have difficulty surviving on the more open and vulnerable rock garden.

The walls of the Alpine Yard shelter a number of interesting shrubs. On the inside, the beautifully scented yellow flowers of the Chinese *Chimonanthus praecox* are produced before the leaves in February. A climbing form of the rose, 'Cécile Brünner' produces blossoms throughout the summer and into the late autumn. Tender shrubs and herbs survive and even thrive in the warmer microclimate of this enclosed space.

opposite: Alpine House

THE WATER HOUSE, SUCCULENT HOUSE AND FERN HOUSE

above: Inside the Killarney Fern House

above: *Echinocactus grusonii* below: *Opuntia vulgaris*

This curious trio of glasshouses were built at different times and in different materials and, as a result, they fit together somewhat uncomfortably.

The oldest, dating to 1854, is the Water House. It was built in cast and wrought iron to grow the giant Amazonian waterlily (*Victoria amazonica*). The waterlily had been introduced to cultivation in 1846 and was certainly the botanical sensation of that decade.

The wooden succulent house was built at the end of the 19th century. A range of cacti and other succulents adapted to drought and hot desert conditions are grown. The plant collection illustrates the evolution of different plant families in response to harsh desert environments.

At odds with its 19th century companions is the 1960's, aluminium-frame, Fern House. Tropical and other non-hardy ferns and fern-allies are grown. Some of the species in the house, including the Australian and New Zealand tree ferns, survive happily outdoors in the more lush gardens in the South-West of Ireland and in coastal gardens elsewhere in Ireland.

opposite: *Victoria amazonica* Inset: Two day old flower

THE GREAT PALM HOUSE

above: *Livistonia*
right: *Encephalartos altensteinii*
bottom: Re-potting in the Palm House in 1999

So named to distinguish it from the older central palm house of the Curvilinear Range, the Great Palm House was prefabricated by Boyds of Paisley, near Glasgow. It was erected during the winter of 1883-1884 after an earlier wooden palm house had been badly damaged in a gale. The house has walls of teak and roof glazing bars of wrought iron. Work in preparation for a restoration of the house has been in progress since 1999.

The Great Palm House contains rare cycads as well as tropical palms, bamboo, bananas, crinums and bromeliads, as well as a varied collection of tropical plants from around the world.

opposite: Great Palm House

THE ORCHID HOUSE

Orchids have a special place in the Glasnevin story. It was here in the 1840's that orchids were first grown to flowering stage from seed by the Curator, David Moore. Frederick Moore continued his father's interest in tropical orchids and assembled an outstanding collection of species orchids for which Glasnevin was justly famous. A renewal of interest in tropical orchids has resulted from a number of expeditions to Belize in Central America in recent years. Restoration of the Orchid House is planned in tandem with the Palm House.

above: *Masdevallia coccinea* 'Harryana'

left: *Laelia anceps* 'Alba'
below: *Dendrobium nobile*

right: *Encyclia cochleata*

Plant Conservation

The National Botanic Gardens, Glasnevin, assists in promoting an awareness of biological diversity and the need to conserve the flora of the world and the rich heritage of cultivated plants.

The National Botanic Gardens works closely with the Wildlife Research section of Dúchas and with the Universities and voluntary bodies on plant conservation projects. A number of native Irish plants have been protected under the Wildlife Act since 1976. Some of these are grown at the National Botanic Gardens together with other rare native species. Artificial habitats have been constructed to extend the range of plants grown. These include a small replica of the limestone pavement of the Burren.

Conservation of garden plants is promoted by the National Botanic Gardens. Cultivated varieties which originated in Ireland or have special significance for the country are grown and distributed. These plants have been listed and described in Dr. Charles Nelson's book, 'A Heritage of Beauty', published by the Irish Garden Plant Society. The Gardens works with the Society (IGPS) and with the National Council for the Conservation of Plants and Gardens (NCCPG) in conserving the biological diversity which has been selected and maintained for centuries by the art of the gardener.

CITES, the Convention on International Trade in Endangered Species, also known as the Washington Convention, has been adopted by the European Union. It regulates trade in endangered plant and animal species. In Ireland CITES is administered by Dúchas The Heritage Service (Department of Arts, Heritage, Gaeltacht and the Islands).

left: The rare native plant
Ajuga pyramidalis
below: The cultivated
variety *Escallonia* 'C.F. Ball'

EDUCATION AT THE GARDENS

Part of the purpose of the National Botanic Gardens is to promote the study of plants and planting. Visitors can learn about plants at the Gardens by studying the themed displays, by taking guided tours and by reading the labels. The Guide Service promotes school visits, which are free of charge. Teachers are encouraged to prepare for visits by contacting the Gardens in advance to discuss the programme and level of presentation required. Short familiarisation courses for teachers are conducted at the Gardens.

Teagasc, the State body with responsibility for education and research in agriculture and horticulture, conducts a formal course in Amenity Horticulture at the Gardens.

above: Children making a bark rubbing

The three-year course leads to a Diploma in Horticulture. The Teagasc course continues a tradition of horticultural education at Glasnevin that goes back to 1812, when the first apprentices were taken on.

above: Teagasc students planting the Carpet bedding

THE NATIONAL HERBARIUM

The Herbarium contains over half a million dried and documented plant specimens that are filed in special metal cabinets and easily accessed for study. The herbarium collections include all the plant groups and the fungi and are divided into two sections, the native Irish collections and plants from the rest of the world. Herbarium specimens provide easily accessed samples of each plant species or variety, type specimens for plant names and a record of the occurrence of a plant at a particular time and place. Specimens provide data and material which cannot be substituted by a photograph or illustration and, although dried and dead, preserve many of the characteristics of the living plant. The herbarium provides much of the basic materials for research on plant classification and nomenclature. It is also an invaluable aid to plant identification.

above: Dried ferns from Sikkim, North East India *photo: D Synnott*

above: Research
right: Herbarium specimens
dating from 1661 *photo: J Scarry*

The Herbarium also contains a large collection of fruits, seeds, wood, fibres, plant extracts and artefacts which are part of the collections of the museum of economic botany begun by the Dublin Society (now the Royal Dublin Society) and supplemented by additions at the Gardens and the National Museum of Ireland. The Herbarium collection is housed in a new building, purpose built for the herbarium and library collections.

THE LIBRARY

Formed by the amalgamation of the library at the Gardens with that of the Herbarium when it was transferred from the National Museum in 1970, the Library contains an estimated forty thousand items. The oldest volume is the 1532 Brunfels' Herbal. Other interesting books include a 1597 edition of Gerard's Herbal and many early 19th century illustrated floras many of which were donated by the eccentric but successful gardener William Gumbleton of Cork.

The Library is a working one serving staff, students and bona fide researchers. It is not open to the general public but tours and exhibitions are arranged from time to time. Every effort is made to stay abreast of the available

above: Inside the Library

literature on taxonomic botany and practical horticulture. Over three hundred journals are current. Many are acquired through exchange for Glasra, Notes from the National Botanic Gardens, Glasnevin, and other occasional publications from the Gardens.

above left: Frontispiece to Sibthorp's *Flora Graeca* (1806) *photo: J Scarry*
above right: Frontispiece to Brunfels' Herbal (1532) *photo: J Scarry*

The collections of botanical art, mostly original watercolour illustrations of flowering plants and fungi, are stored away from the light in a controlled environment. They are exhibited as opportunities allow.